SPIRITUAL ENLIGHTMENT

A COLLECTION OF CONTEMPORARY POEMS

EDWARD HAYES

ISBN 979-8-88832-037-2 (paperback)
ISBN 979-8-88832-038-9 (digital)

Christian Faith Publishing
832 Park Avenue
Meadville, PA 16335
www.christianfaithpublishing.com

Printed in the United States of America

In loving memory of Uncle Saul, 1934–2023

God's Love

God loves us
regardless of what we do
Even on rainy days—
the sunrays will
shine through
Thank HIM
for HIS blessings
every day

Bro. Hayes
March 24, 2022

God Is Real!

God is real, so I can feel HIM in my soul
I'm not dreaming feeling God's love
Oh! My heavenly Father forgives me for my earthly sins
And transgressions
Sometimes I fall short as backsliders often do,
Not living as a Christian ought being obedient to divine order
Don't need to knock on wood,
Or place a bet on sporting numbers
How can you lose with God on your side?
As a true believer,
I cannot play hide-and-seek with my faith in the God unseen
I know my God is real—
Because of the power of prayer, I managed to overcome my fears,
No matter what I say or do,
I still receive an abundance of blessings, love, and tranquility
My God never forsaken me

Bro. Hayes
March 24, 2022

Help Me Make It to Daylight

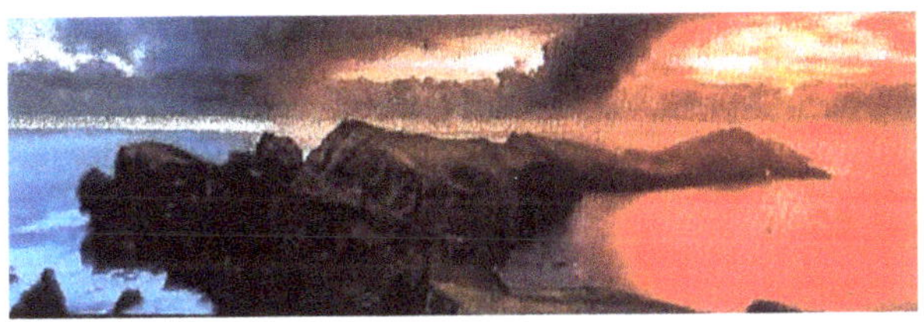

Stars trickling, shining so bright
Far, far away in heavenly delight
Please help me make it through the night
Ghastly ghosts and goblins lie in wait,
Demons awake, controlling my dreamlike sleep
I tossed and turned a thousand sleepless nights
Waiting for the daylight
Alas! I can almost escape my demons' plight
A drink or two on liquor's breath—
I'm anticipating getting through the night to rest
When daylight comes
And the sun creeps across the horizon,
I'll know I've won another day
In the daylight

Bro Hayes
January 16, 2022

Fix Me, Lord, Fix Me!

Fix me, Lord, fix me!
This isn't exactly the way the lyrics was written
But our Lord and Savior will forgive the purpose intended
Giving honor and glory to God for mankind's repentance

Fix me, Lord, fix me!
Now some of y'all don't like giving up the old religious songs,
Listening to the new drummer's beats
Shouting in the church's aisles seemingly like a disco thing
Do not affect your faith in God

Fix me, Lord, fix me!
When I am feeling sad and blue, lonely and downhearted—
Lord, lend us a helping hand to fix what's wrong with humanity.
I peeked over the mountainside and didn't like the view
Too much evil in this old world without a blemish on religion

Fix me, Lord, fix me!
When catastrophes block our way ahead
The sun is not shining on rainy days
Forgetting that Jesus suffered as the forgotten Son,
Carrying a heavy cross up Calvary's hill
So mankind can be forgiven for our sins for eternity

Fix me, Lord, fix me!
Some of us read the Bible
To reminisce about what Jesus and His disciples did;
Along came the Four Horsemen of the Apocalypse
Written in Revelations scriptures…
News of the rapture still explains why faith is needed

Fix me! Fix me! Fix me, Lord, fix me!
It said that prayer is the pathway to salvation
To see our way through and joy cometh in the morning
How many times does the Almighty have to prove his love?
His eyes are on the sparrow;
I know He rewards us for our obedience to the divine laws
And living by the golden rule

Bro. Hayes
March 11, 2022

Sacred Scripture Found in the Twenty-Third Psalms

O Lord, on bended knees, I praise your holy name
For the sacred things revealed in the twenty-third Psalms,
In six biblical verses, written in the King James Bible

First, the Lord is the Shepherd of the flock of mankind,
He showers us every day with His blessings
Second, He comforts us in time of need
Encourages us to enjoy greener pastures besides still waters,
He's a mighty force to be reckoned with for the nonbelievers
Third, He restoreth our soul when righteousness takes over
Preparing the true believers for the kingdom of glory
Fourth, I walk through the valley of death and fear no evil,
Our Lord protects thee;
A calamity of our earthly deeds will be unyielded,
Most important words spoken by the preacher
At the graveside at our homecomings
Fifth, Jesus Christ, the blood of the Lamb,
Died for the sins of humanity
Giving honor to the Most High God—
My cup runneth over with goodness and mercy
Sixth, my charitable works serving humanity
May not be recorded in the historical annals;
Doing God's bidding will surely be counted
And I will dwell in the Lord's house forever and ever
Amen!

Bro. Hayes
May 1, 2022

Why Does It Matter

Why does it matter
Seems like reality is a false narrative
"Society has grown cold, bitter, and mean"

In this old world, we're losing our perspective to dream—
Nothing seems to matter, not even the little things
Nowadays it's blasphemous if you call your God by name

In our Christian teachings
We were taught to honor and obey our parents
As one of the Ten Commandments etched in stone
But this society don't respect our elders
It appears the goal is to destroy each other
And disrespect our neighbors

Why does it matter
If all of a sudden humanity becomes color-blind,
Following the heavenly Father's instructions
Accepting divine law as our guide
When mankind discovers the true meanings of brotherly love

Bro. Hayes
August 31, 2022

Interpretation of the Twenty-Third Psalms

In the beginning, the Lord is my Shepherd
And he watches over me—
He comforts me without pause
Encourages me to sit beside still waters,
In greener pastures, believing in my God unseen

He restoreth my soul through trouble times,
In my Christian teachings, we prepare to
Enter into the kingdom of glory

For I walk through the shadow of death
Fearing no evil, death is inevitable—
It's an immortal sleep under God's directions
Let His will be done without objection

Surely, we all have a date with the grim reaper;
No one escapes life except through death, regardless of riches,
Skin tones, or religious beliefs

I would like to walk with Jesus like Ezekiel, the prophet did
Celebrating the salvation of humanity
Giving honor to the Most High God, bestowing His blessings
And allowing my cup to runneth over with goodness and mercy

When this life's journey has ended and my race won—
I have to be accountable for what I've done,
Realizing the power of prayer for forgiveness
And repentance of my sins and transgressions
Like Jesus, I tried to do God's biddings
To gain admission in my heavenly home

Bro. Hayes
May 1, 2022

Religion Is a Song

The doubters and haters, bet I couldn't create a poem
Using Old Tyme Religious songs when I ascend Jabbor's ladder
To my brand-new heavenly home. It has many rooms in His mansion
Sitting beside the Father on His throne: "Ain't That Good News?"

When the angels meet in the skies and talk about the passenger's list
    for glory;
It's written in the thirteenth Psalms: "Joy cometh in the morning."
I have no doubt that the "The Victory Is Mine," Jesus died for the
    sins of the world
On Calvary's hill: "Take My Hand, Precious Lord."

Let the church say amen—
Reminder of Peter who betrayed our Lord
And was beheaded for denying he knew Jesus three times,
Even though they crucified my Lord: "Can't No Grave Hold My
    Body Down."

Whenever I am feeling down and bewildered,
I ask for His blessings: "Fix Me, Jesus" until things get better.
"Will the Circle Be Unbroken?"
Reciting our daily prayers, it's so good that we sing it as a gospel hymn
Explaining His tender mercies and goodness.

Comin' up over the "Rough Side of the Mountain,"
Can't go any further without God's instructions.
It's a hidden secret, like where the prophets are buried,
We look to the heavens for guidance by "His Eye Is on the Sparrow."

Now that we've discovered that prayer is the pathway to salvation,
"I'm Taking Back What the Devil Stole from Me."
Journey down the winding stairs of life: "Hallelujah."
Giving honor to God and all the glory.

Bro. Hayes
April 15, 2022

A Spiritual Check

This is a spiritual check of epic proportions
If I asked the moral majority
have y'all prayed today
I've probably lost the bet
unless you haven't lost faith in righteousness
What's old is new again
and new holds secrets untold
Now we don't know what's up ahead
but it ain't looking good for brighter days
If mankind doesn't change their evil ways
Darker days will surely prevail
How can the light shine through this twisted
thing called humanity
But until then, I'll keep my faith in my God
Through divine intervention and prayer
all things are possible.

Bro. Hayes
March 15, 2022

Fantasy Gone Wild

People of earth
Are we traveling on a crash course of no return
To our imaginary designation of disillusionment—
Fantasy gone wild

Perhaps we, as humans, are headed on a galactic journey far, far away,
To an abyss of spacelessness, unrestrictive indulgence, and escapism
Where time is a microcosm of our earthly endeavors and shattered
    dreams

In this make believe, universal equation,
Time is not a sequential measurement of days, months, or years
Rather, it holds man accountable for his proclaimed hypocrisy
To treat all men equally as brothers

Sooner, rather than later,
Perhaps light years away
Mankind will enter into a perfect Utopia
Where sex, color, creed, or religious affinity don't matter
It's the content of the person's character that wins

Fantasy gone wild is a harsh reality
That this society must do better—
To avoid this crash course we're headed
Without divine intervention, there's no perfect Utopia

Bro Hayes
March 21, 2022

Greatness Is Our Weakness

Are we being disingenuous
  Downplaying our greatness
   Empathizing our weakness
The so-called doers and takers
   Looking for clues in the rearview mirror
Showing off our ugliness in public places
   Hiding our goodness behind the scenes
Neglecting to tell truths about lifetime successes
    And failures
It's about time mankind realizes, without spirituality
   Religion has a blemish on its record
There is no heaven without hell
   Good without evil
Spread an abundant of love amongst humanity
   Like the Creator intended
The Christians believe in God unseen
   Nonbelievers the existence of the devil
    Lucifer the deceiver

Bearer of light, taking ownership of souls
        Of the very wicked hateful-minded people
Be cautious of the light you're seeking
        When darkness prevails
                Hindering a walk-in faith
                    Blinding our sight for salvation
Are we being disingenuous
        Reevaluating expectations
                For the human race existence

Bro. Hayes
May 19, 2022

Is It Right to Play God?

Is it right for man to play God
The question is whether it's right to save a life
That's nearly at the end without medical intervention

Being a medical surgeon
You removed a heart and internal organs without permission
Knowing you might face legal charges and lose your license
To save other patient's lives are worth it

Your love one was diagnosed with an incurable cancer
There's no hope for recovery; prayer ain't changing their condition
Y'all are tired of seeing them suffer,
The family tells the doctor to remove the breathing apparatus

What if you're in a fender bender
And the other driver has road rage and psychological deficiencies
An argument ensues, and he shoots you
Your life flashes before your face—
The medics arrive, trying to revive you

Playing God to save a life in certain situations is a necessity
Otherwise, as advertised, it's a legal issue
Perhaps this is an abomination of Christian values
The Almighty allows man to make free decisions,
Putting the scalpel's blade in the hands of a skilled surgeon
To save a life creates a moral dilemma

Bro. Hayes
April 6, 2022

Losing a Loved One

Sometimes when sadness comes our way
Losing a loved one that was one of our favorites
We pray for God to take the pain away
And comfort us for brighter days

God makes no mistakes calling them home to glory,
Sometimes we question the reasoning
Forgetting their final race has been won—
No mo' pains, suffering, or sorrows

One day, when our time comes,
We will reunite with loved ones passed away
Seeing family members behind the pearly gates
What a wonderful homecoming

But until then, we will keep them in remembrance,
Keep smiling and uplifted in prayer
Remembering those cherished memories time to time,
"Joy cometh in the morning"

Bro Hayes
August 20, 2022

Places I Wish I Could've Been!
A Sermon

My inspiration comes from my Christian faith from within to tell
    mankind,
What's needed is a spiritual awakening and the goodness of our
    Creator
If so, I could relive in biblical times and the places I wish I could've been
Speaking directly with the heavenly Father

I wish I could've been where Moses stood,
In front of the burning bush with the everlasting flames
When God spoke to Moses, "Remove thy sandals from beneath thy feet,
You're standing on holy ground
I summoned you here to give you the Ten Commandments written
    in stone;
For the children of Israel to obey and live forever in eternity"
But their sinfulness paved their way, so they disobeyed
Wandering in the desert sands for forty years
Never reaching the promised land

I wish I could've been there when Abraham signed the covenant with
    God
The Almighty promised that his seeds would produce many nations;
This was his reward for being obedient and living by the divine laws
As a test of faith! God sent an angel, instructing Abraham to sacrifice
    Isaac,
His beloved son on Mount Moriah, as a burnt offering. Without pause,
Abraham did as God instructed, and Isaac was spared as promised

Places I wish I could've been with the prophets that did God's bidding;
Amos, Ezekiel, Jeremiah, Malachi, and Muhammad, just to name a few
They came to inform the multitudes of sinners that the Messiah was
    coming
And repentance of their sinful ways

This earth and heavenly skies wasn't created by an optical illusion,
Simply because we pray to a higher power we cannot see—
That which isn't made by man makes the sun and moon rise and set,
The harmony of birds chirping, rainbows filling the skies, flowers
    blossoming,
And greener things growing in Mother Earth
Picturesque waterfalls that capture nature's splendor

If I had my wish for a rightful place to be at the end of life's journey
Sitting on His throne with the heavenly Father,
The Creator of the universe that makes all things possible

Bro. Hayes
March 15, 2022

WAWAD
(What Are We All Doing)

Tell me what we're all doing before we're through
When there's no more light, only darkness will do

It's an uphill struggle, living today on life's terms
Human decency and respect is a foregone conclusion
Can't change one's skin tones
I guess, intelligence will illuminate the future

Society is so uptight
Got a nasty disposition, not doing what's right
What if this old world is on the rebound?
Not by the hands of the foolish man

You know we ain't there yet
When dreams are shattered into a thousand pieces
Hope is outta sight
Reality, what's missing
We need to close the gates of hell
Say prayer is the pathway to salvation

Go to school, get a higher education
Especially for the darker races
Supremacists' shootings protected by the constitution
Using assault weapons to explain their future—
But never ever let anyone kill your ambitions

Just think of the jubilation
When society has accepted the challenge
That all men are created equal and no longer invisible
Simply, mankind needs a spiritual awakening

Tell me what we're all doing before we're through
When there's no more darkness
And the light shines through

Bro Hayes
June 5, 2022

Living in a Tree House

I'd like to be an eagle
Flying high, soaring with accurate precision in blue skies
Building a nest in a selected tree—
My tree house would be a magnificent specimen
So high to see; that way no one bothers me
Except once a year on special occasions
I can tolerate a few visitors getting away from nosy neighbors
Family that spreads vicious gossip
Not knowing if they're hurting somebody,
All are welcome, but few are invited
We all have family members that did us proud
But some members had violated family's principles
Deserving to be despised, removed from tradition
Christian values teach us to forgive persons that harm us
You may call me selfish and lonely

Living a lifestyle that don't meet your standards,
Simply because I choose to be a hermit
It's not illegal or a mortal sin to demand to be left alone
Living in a Treehouse I call home

I am just saying!

Bro. Hayes
May 8, 2022

Flying Thirty Thousand Feet

Have you ever flown thirty-thousand feet
In the friendly skies,
Southbound on a delayed flight

Sitting on the tarmac for several hours
Much needed vacation now in jeopardy
If the plane doesn't leave the gate

While in flight, I looked out the window
Saw magnificent soapy white clouds,
Covering canopy skies, like the deep blue oceans
You could dream of endless possibilities
And be thankful for experiencing the sightings
Far away on the horizon

Never ever saw another plane while in flight
Or another ship at sea, cruising the Caribbean Islands
Not until we landed or docked near civilization

I must admit that I was scared
The plane dropped a few feet under turbulent winds,
Then I prayed and trusted in the Lord
To take control of the plane until we landed safely.

Bro. Hayes
April 12, 2022

Don't Be so Judgmental!

Just the other day, my neighbor knocks on my door
Asked if he could borrow a cup of sugar,
It's no problem; we have plenty
My wife keeps tabs on me because of my diabetes

I must admit, sometimes I cheat
By eating lots of unhealthy snacks between meals
My cholesterol level rises
After eating several hefty plates of rice and beans
And lots of pasta, my favorite

Did I see my neighbor standing on the food pantry line?
He's always boasting how well his family is doing
So to avoid embarrassment, I acted like I didn't see him
My suspicious nature won me over, being a nosy fellow,
Are the kids being well fed and treated good?
Can't help wondering what's happening in their home

Now! If this life situation does not apply
Let it alone, you're in the few percentiles with privilege
Don't be so judgmental, thinking you're better
Because your bellies fill, bills paid
Children attending private schools,
Diamonds and furs, an enormous bank account
And you're driving a Mercedes
What will happen when disaster strikes,
And you've lost everything, forgetting life's purpose
Acting like an eagle,
Until your head is buried in the sand, like an ostrich

Bro. Hayes
August 4, 2022

Different Colors

Children of all colors
Playing freely in playgrounds across the nation
Having a good time without interference…
Until the parents and adults stop their playtime
With their selfish inclinations—
Don't play with that child,
They don't belong in our inner circles
What a despicable representation of mankind
When subtle prejudices
Disregards the magnificent beautiful colors
Contained in the rainbow coalition

Bro. Hayes
July 26, 2022

Sucker's Friendship

Some people don't know how to value friendship
Just wanna make your acquaintance

They come with smiley faces and deceitful hearts
Shake hands to hide their hidden agendas
Fronting from the gate
They are only waiting to see what they can get

Being a compassionate person
They're accepted into your inner circle
You allowed them to steal your heart with their quick wit
Only to find out, no matter what you do for them,
It'll never be enough to even the score for their friendship

When y'all first met nearly a decade ago,
They were penniless and an emotional wreck
Breaking your heart after doing them a thousand favors
You who cared about their well-being—
Playing you like a victim without a conscience
In their sucker's game, you don't matter

Now that they're on their feet again
Riding high on their horse, forgetting humble beginnings,
If they ever fall from that fate wall they're building
Looking for this friendship again
I just wanna make their acquaintance

Bro. Hayes
April 17, 2022

The Way of Love

The way you walk with a confident stride
    You could've been a peacock with that swagger
The way you swing your hips
    You could've been the Mozart's Symphony
The way you smell so sweet
    You could've been expensive perfume sold at Macy's
The way you look with that hourglass figure
    You could've replaced Mona Lisa
The way you think on your feet
    You could've added to Einstein's laws of relativity
The way of intimacy behind closed doors
    You could've been a teacher, wrote a schoolbook
The way you speak so softly and gently
    You could've been still waters in a raging storm
The way you stole my heart
    You could've been convicted for lover's thievery
The way you do the things you do keeps love anew
    You could've explained why I am in love with you

Bro. Hayes
May 26, 2022

Something Wrong

Something wrong and bothering me
Each time we meet lately, it gets shorter and shorter
Don't blame it on a few drinks of Hennessy
We used to converse for hours, making future plans
Self-amusing and intoxicating
All of a sudden, we just argue for no reason—
Said you're leaving without explaining

Something is wrong, and you wouldn't admit it
Telling me you gotta put our love on the shelf
You're in a panic mood and not thinking clearly
Headed for the door without an explanation
At least, leaving the job requires a two weeks notification

Something wrong, and you're being evasive
Now that my heart is broken into a thousand pieces…
Cascading tears flowing down my face
Like the mighty Mississippi River
Say a grown man ain't supposed to cry
I don't have a clue how to say goodbye

Something wrong and keeping your love to yourself
Oh yeah! And you've built a wall around your heart
Stuffing your feelings with finesse—
Now you're walking me to my door for selfish reasons
You've never done that before…
So! Give yourself a chance to find new romance
Because I wasn't the one you desired
It takes two to tango; I'll miss what we had forever

Bro. Hayes
April 30, 2022

Unsung Love Affair

Love doesn't live here anymore…
More than twenty years, I've been faithful
Only had a one-night fling being mad at you

I've been around a time or two,
Remember that night when I told the truth
I ain't no Romeo, and you're not Florence Nightingale
Neither one has been true blue in this toxic relation
No matter who's right or wrong—
Sick and tired of harmonizing sad love songs

After trying numerous times to make this love thing work
I'm finished with your smoothing deception,
Lying through your teeth about your infidelity
Frontin' from the gate about the new love you've met
It's painful to leave after years of commitment

My chances are slim to none
Hoping you'll return on your own volition
Now that the kids are grown, you'll be enjoying
Your new found freedom

When you left, I closed the door on romance
Self-medicating to ease the pain
Drinking too much to forget the blues
Being home alone, I nearly went insane
"Only four walls to comfort me"

And if you ever decide to come back, my love
I am willing to try anew;
But I'm no longer volunteering to be a victim of unsung love

Bro. Hayes
January 26, 2022

Chasing!

Say you're chasing things you cannot have or afford
Like the cutie with the fantastic body that moved next door
Knowing nothing about her,
With a pleasing personality and a smile that'll melt butter
You've done this sort of thing plenty times
Not thinking with your head above your shoulders
Interested in her physicality that's blinding
So you say! Just wanted to make her acquaintance
How can you be certain that her intellect
Passes the friendship test
Simply because you got her attention
Perhaps another potential conquest under your belt
After your initial conversation
She says happy to meet you
But isn't interested in your intentions

Just got out of a toxic relationship,
Ex-boyfriend has anger management issues
Had to get a court order to move to safety,
Meanwhile, my kids are staying with my parents
Until I find another job and a new identity
Now, are you sure you wanna make my acquaintance?
Placing yourself in imminent danger
Perhaps you're still chasing

Bro. Hayes
May 1, 2022

Stop Hiding from Yourself!

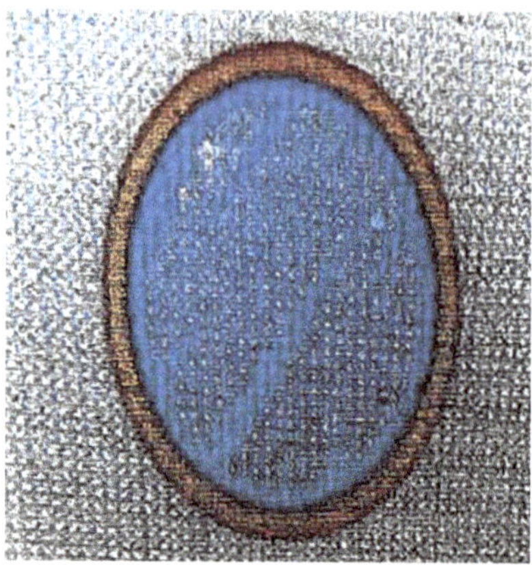

You can't hide from the mirrors on the wall
every glance and stare you'll see yourself
Your fragile ego is bruised
Like a play castle built on a sandy beach
When a strong wind blows, it will surely fall
How are you gonna win?
Fighting with the pains from within
thinking everybody is against you
The truth is stranger than fiction
If I didn't know better
It seems that you're fighting yourself
Now! It's a hurtful thing
admitting one's character flaws
No matter what's said or done

Nothing easy changes overnight
Perhaps, in a lifetime or two
you'll find a clue
Keep looking in the rearview mirrors
It is a stranger gaining on you

Bro. Hayes
March 30, 2022

When Love Was New

The main reason for matrimonial breakups is
blamed on failure to communicate
Couples not revealing their innermost feelings and insecurities
Instead, they make a conscious decision to
say hurtful things to each other,
Misinterpreted their true meanings to their significant other

We've gotten too familiar
Invested the best years of our lives, our love is now in jeopardy
The children are all grown up and moved away
Creating an empty-nest syndrome—
Stayed together all of those years for the sake of the kids
The adults in the room soon discover
they have even less in common

The problem isn't that we didn't talk or love each other
We stopped paying attention to the little things that mattered
What derailed our marriage was lack of
respect, neglect, and appreciation
Spent too many nights not knowing if you were alive or dead
Sleeping alone in a king-size bed

Say! We have irreconcilable differences
Neither one wanted to give an inch
Failure to set boundaries was a recipe for disaster
To sustain a loving relationship

Let's start anew
If you're willing to save the matrimonial vows,
Counseling is needed to save the marriage the second time around
It doesn't matter who was right or wrong

Bro. Hayes
March 25, 2022

Looking for Love

Goodness gracious, looking for love in all the wrong places
Searching between heaven and earth with endless possibilities

Perhaps, if you look harder, you'll find love in front of your face
We can enjoy a *chatilla* of love's semantics and ecstasy

Past affairs have failed giving you pause
It's time to check your emotional baggage
In the Heartbreak Hotel
Nothing ventures, and nothing gains,
Remain in a rut with a broken heart
And ego bruises

Change your name to hide the shame
Buy new clothing to change your appearance
This doesn't improve your image

But until love resurfaced again
You'll need an attitude adjustment—
Few will notice that love ain't perfect

Bro. Hayes
April 20, 2022

Life's Conundrums

The older I get
    more critical of little things
        neglecting their importance
I realized lesser days ahead
    getting myself in order for the final race
The thought of my wisdom amassed
        things I've seen are frightening
I've succumbed to the knowledge of self-prophecy
    still a work in progress
"Miles to go before I sleep"
        recalibrated my moral compass
Taking sunny views with those who disagrees
    no one is right all the time
        or perfect
The longer I live, the more irrelevant
    I've become
Let my lifetime works speak for my relevancy

Bro Hayes
August 1, 2022

If I Was in Charge

If I was in charge of this world gone mad
It would be a perfect oasis
Where all men are truly free
Kindness and love prevail
It's a crying shame this mess man has made

My world so fine,
You'll be foolish not to come inside
I would declare a holiday all week long
Presenting an equal opportunity for all races
No more struggle to make ends meet
Financing wars for political propaganda,
No more racial tensions escalated by hatred,
For the sake of the silent majority
We must do our fair share of self-introspection

Every day would be sunny,
It's no longer a need to chase that paper
No more lying and cheating
Stop gun violence to further racial agendas
Banned assault weapons
Only cupid shoots arrows for the love seekers

Every little boy and girl would get an education
Tucked safely in bed with their bellies fed
Teaching them the power of payers

The decadence and human vile that's destroying this nation,
Demand society to reveal their redemptive qualities
To save humanity

Bro. Hayes
June 6, 2022

Congratulations on Your Wedding Day

This is one of the most memorable days,
Recorded as a proclamation in the family's legacy
Deciding to become husband and wife,
May y'all live for a lifetime happily ever

Your love for each other will be on display
For family and friends
Coming from near and far
To share in this momentous occasion

Starting life's journey as a couple
When two hearts beat as one
Sharing a lifetime with your soulmate;
No greater gift sharing with a special person

This reunion is sanctioned by a Higher Power
Always honor and cherish your matrimonial vows
Love endureth all things thought impossible—
Trust in the Lord to lead the way
When you pray for a successful marriage

May you live each day fulfilling life's purpose
Now and then, reflect on your wedding day
And the reasons why you got married

Edward Hayes
June 25, 2022

Tribute on Father's Day

This is a tribute to fathers everywhere,
A special day that family and friends share
Fatherhood is the acknowledgment of
        the family's legacy;
You're the rock the family depends on for
        guidance and protection
Without your seed, there's no generations
        to follow
Give yourself a pat on the back,
        another year of survival
Perhaps you'll get socks and underwear
        Or an expensive gift, finances permitting
Just know that it's not the size or cost
        of the gift that counts
Given in earnest from the heart
        The love and affection
        for those who care

Wife is happy, kids are safe, bills paid
     A few dollars left over for savings
Let no one rain on your parade on this
        momentous occasion
I am honored to be called father,
     my joy comes from being your dad
Your presence is worthy of celebrating,
     The importance in the family's structure;
Happy Father's Day

Bro. Hayes
June 19, 2022

An Adult Nursery Rhythm

It's a foregone conclusion living in this society
you'd rather be an eagle instead of a pigeon
You can boast about being a lion
King of the jungle
Living without an identity
Being sheepish isn't on the menu
    Luckily, you not the eighteenth dinner guest
    of Jeffrey Dahmer
Ain't nothing funny surviving the concrete jungle
If you're the wrong color
    Say the starting line is color-blind
        People of color is being left out of the race of
        humankind
Society should be ashamed of the human vile
    Treating the darker races as cowardly lions
        They don't know the agony and pain
        broken dreams of the downtrodden
If I had to do it all over again
    I'll come back as a human
        Only then, humanity will realize
        that the darker races is one of God's creations

Bro. Hayes
April 26, 2022

Sick and Tired of Bad Behavior

I'm sick and tired of excusing bad behavior
By people not setting or respecting boundaries,
Tired of being told to take the proverbial high ground
Excusing grown folks who knows better

The breakdown of long-standing reunions
Is not the avoidance of setting boundaries.
It's the infringement
When people assume it's all right to take liberties

Now we were all taught right from wrong;
The biggest crock is when people say they're trying to do better!
Trying to sell ice to the Eskimos during winter

Society must shoulder its share of blame
Succumbing to the human vile, decadence, and shame
Reflections of the madding crowd that losing their humanity

Unfortunately, there's no prosthesis for rudeness or disrespect,
Speaking about infringement of one's personal space,
People usually takes kindness for weakness
Masquerading under the guise of friendship

This false image we're proclaiming doesn't excuse bad behavior—
Blame failed relationships on blurred communications…
The solution to address this issue
Is the acceptance of other boundaries
By listening to what's being said by the persons being disrespected

Bro. Hayes
September 8, 2022

About the Author

Edward Hayes is a New York City worker retiree. Writing has been one of the things on his long-term bucket list. After his retirement, the urge to continue writing became a priority and compassion.

He doesn't consider himself a poet; rather, he is a writer that expresses his narratives through poetic writings. More importantly, his creativity comes from my spiritual perspective and belief in God. In some regards, he thinks of himself as a realist and open-minded individual. Given the dynamics of the human vile, decadence, racial discord, and gun violence that exists in today's society, he has to believe in divine intervention and prayer as the pathway to saving humanity.